THE BATTLE OVER SLAVERY

Causes and Effects of the U.S. Civil War

BY MICHAEL CAPEK

Consultant:
Lyde Cullen Sizer, PhD
Professor of U.S. Cultural and Intellectual History
Sarah Lawrence College
Bronxville, New York

CAPSTONE PRESS
a capstone imprint

Connect is published by Capstone Press,
1710 Roe Crest Drive, North Mankato, Minnesota 56003
www.capstonepub.com

Library of Congress Cataloging-in-Publication Data
Capek, Michael.
  The battle over slavery : causes and effects of the U.S. Civil War / by Michael Capek.
      pages cm.—(Connect. The Civil War)
  Summary: "The Civil War began when Confederate troops attacked Fort Sumter.
But years of tension led to that battle. And the war would prove to have major
consequences for both sides. Explore the causes and effects of the Civil War—a war to
determine the future of the United States. Perfect for Common Core studies on cause
and effect relationships"—Provided by publisher.
  Includes bibliographical references and index.
  ISBN 978-1-4914-2009-6 (library binding)
  ISBN 978-1-4914-2162-8 (paperback)
  ISBN 978-1-4914-2168-0 (ebook PDF)
1. United States—History—Civil War, 1861–1865—Juvenile literature. I. Title.
  E468.C243 2015
  973.7'11—dc23   2014023657

Editorial Credits
Adrian Vigliano, editor; Veronica Scott, designer; Wanda Winch, media researcher;
Kathy McColley, production specialist

Photo Credits
Bridgeman Images: ©Look and Learn/Private Collection/Andrew Howat, cover;
Capstone, 6; CriaImages.com: Jay Robert Nash Collection, 4-5 (background); Getty
Images: Fotosearch, 8-9 (all), 39, Interim Archives, 34-35, Kean Collection, 22-23, MPI,
16; The Granger Collection, 10, 13, 17, 18 (back), 20, 37; Library of Congress: Prints
and Photographs Division, 4 (middle), 11, 14 (m), 18 (m), 19, 21, 22 (bottom), 24, 25,
27, 28-33, 36, 38, 40-45; North Wind Picture Archives, 7, 13 (b), Shutterstock: Ekaterina
Romanova (ornate frame), Ensuper (multi color background), Extezy (vintage
calligraphy design), f-f-f-f (décor calligraphy elements), GarryKillian (damask design),
Lucy Baldwin (grunge rust texture), nikoniano (stripes pattern), wacomka (floral
pattern); Superstock: Everett Collection, 14-15 (map); www.historicalimagebank.com
Painting by Don Troiani, 26

Printed in the United States of America in Stevens Point, Wisconsin.
092014   008479WZS15

TABLE OF CONTENTS

The Civil War was the worst war ever fought on American soil. Shooting started in April 1861. The fighting did not stop until April 1865. During that time, Americans fought one another in battle after bloody battle. When the war was over, billions of dollars worth of property had been damaged. Worse, at least 620,000 soldiers had died. Some historians believe that number may be closer to 750,000. And these numbers do not even count civilian deaths.

How did the war get started? What made fellow citizens, neighbors, and even family members take different sides and start fighting one another? The Civil War had several causes. But the main issue, slavery, was present at the very beginning.

Civil War battlefields were the scenes of many deadly fights between the North and the South.

American War Deaths

Revolutionary War
(1775–1783)
about 7,200

World War I
(1914–1918)
about 116,500

World War II
(1939–1945)
about 400,000

Korean War and Vietnam War
(1954–1975)
about 94,500

Fact

The Civil War claimed more lives than any other American war.

WHAT CAUSED THE CIVIL WAR?

Cause #1

THE SLAVERY ISSUE

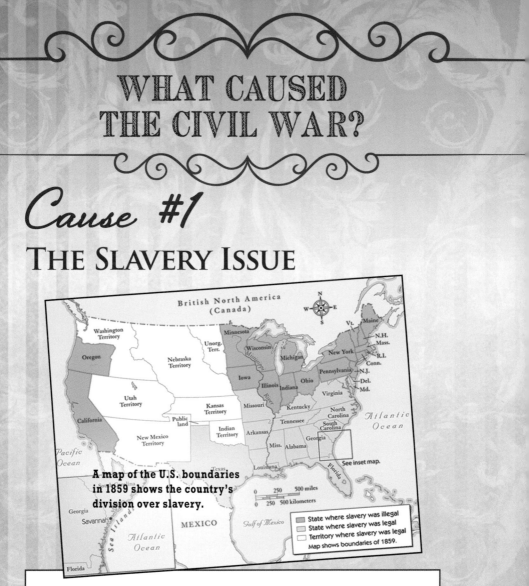

British North America
(Canada)

A map of the U.S. boundaries in 1859 shows the country's division over slavery.

0   250   500 miles
0   250   500 kilometers

State where slavery was illegal
State where slavery was legal
Territory where slavery was legal
Map shows boundaries of 1859.

In 1775 nearly 500,000 slaves lived in the North American colonies. By the early 1800s the number of slaves had grown to over 700,000. They were either newly captured Africans or the descendents of African slaves who were already here.

The U.S. Constitution went into effect in 1788. By 1800 slavery had been mostly abolished in Northern states. A law passed in 1807 banned bringing in new slaves. But the number of slaves continued to grow. By 1860, nearly 4 million slaves lived in the United States.

The debate over slavery was already present at the time of the founding of the United States. Those who opposed slavery often pointed to the Declaration of Independence. They argued that its words about rights and equality applied to black people as well as whites.

"We hold these truths to be self-evident, that all men are created equal, that they are endowed by their Creator with certain unalienable Rights, that among these are Life, Liberty and the pursuit of Happiness."

—*The Declaration of Independence, adopted July 4, 1776*

Slaves suffered terrible crowded conditions on ships bound for the United States.

Most white people in the South did not own slaves, homes, or land. The idea of owning property, including slaves, was appealing to them, but few had any hope of that ever happening. Still, most white Southerners benefited from slave labor. The work slaves did made their owners and states they lived in very rich.

Most slaves lived, worked, and died on large farms called **plantations**. Slaves grew crops such as rice, cotton, and tobacco. Harvesting these crops, especially cotton, was brutal work. It had to be done by hand, bending over in the intense heat of the Southern climate. Plantation owners often forced their slaves to work 14 or more hours a day during planting and harvest seasons.

Plowing rice fields was back-breaking work.

plantation—a large farm found in warm areas; before the Civil War, plantations in the South used slave labor

Not every slave harvested crops. Some were overseers or plantation managers. Others worked as blacksmiths, bricklayers, master carpenters, chefs, bakers, and weavers. Slaves also served the public by maintaining roads and buildings.

From the very young to the very old, slaves were expected to work hard on plantations.

Abolitionists spoke out against the use of slaves in the South.

Slavery was based on the idea of **white supremacy.** In the early 1800s, while many Northern whites disliked slavery, they still didn't believe blacks were their equals. Many whites felt slavery was good or natural for black people.

Some Americans believed in ending slavery. These people began a campaign to convince the American public of the evils of slavery. In 1833 the **abolitionist** American Anti-Slavery Society was organized. Forceful leaders such as William Lloyd Garrison spoke and wrote about the need to end slavery immediately. Abolitionist ideas were not popular, however, in the North or the South. Abolitionists were often attacked and their materials burned. It would take time for Northerners to think differently about slavery.

white supremacy—the idea that the white race is superior to all other races
abolitionist—a person who worked to end slavery before the Civil War

The Fugitive Slave Act of 1850

After years of free and slave states arguing over new territories, Congress passed the **Compromise** of 1850. Politicians hoped to satisfy both sides with the five bills contained in the Compromise. One of the bills was a new **Fugitive** Slave Act. The Fugitive Slave Act said that runaway slaves found in the North had to be returned to their owners. Northern abolitionists were outraged. Some people chose to break the law and help slaves escape rather than send them back.

This drawing from 1850 shows a group of white men attacking suspected runaway slaves in a cornfield.

compromise—to agree to something that is not exactly what you wanted in order to make a decision
fugitive—someone who has escaped from prison or slavery

IN CRUEL BONDAGE

Slavery was a nightmarish experience for black people. Captured Africans were packed like cargo in the holds of ships. The journey across the Atlantic could last as long as four months. Those who survived the trip were herded like animals to markets. Plantation owners bid high prices for the strongest and healthiest. Many buyers and sellers did not care if slave families were separated. Slaves who tried to run away or fight back were beaten, chained, or caged. Many slave traders became rich capturing people in Africa and selling them in America.

Slave homes were usually small, rough huts. Many people lived in each one. Workdays were long and hard. Slaves had no free choices about their own lives. They also had little hope that things would ever get much better.

Still, many slaves fought back or took the great risk of trying to escape. In 1831 a slave named Nat Turner led a rebellion in Virginia. The rebellion was stopped after a few days and Turner was eventually hanged along with more than 50 of his followers. Since violent resistance was dangerous, many slaves found safer ways to protest. Some broke or hid farm tools and equipment. When no one was looking, others set fires or damaged their master's possessions. Some worked slowly, pretended to be ill, or did poor-quality work.

Fact

Children born to slave mothers were considered slaves. This happened whether or not their fathers were free.

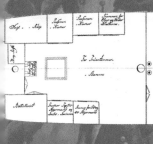

Captured Africans were arranged like cargo on slave ships.

Cause #2
WESTWARD EXPANSION AND STATES' RIGHTS

In this engraving from 1853, a man reacts to news of the Mexican War.

During the first half of the 1800s, America grew at an incredible rate. Between 1803 and 1845 the nation nearly tripled in size. The Mexican War (1846–1848) added another huge section of land to the United States. The treaty that ended the war gave the United States much of the West, including California.

All of this new territory created new opportunities. But it also created huge problems. Slave states wanted to share in the development of the new territories. Many Southern leaders claimed the right to bring slaves into new territories. They also argued for states' rights. Southerners wanted states to have more freedom to make decisions with less interference from the federal government. Many Northern leaders were just as determined to stop the Southern "Slave Power" from spreading slavery. The argument over states' rights and the power of the federal government continued to grow.

A pro-slavery group from Missouri attacks a group of Kansas settlers.

As new states entered the Union, leaders tried to keep a balance between new "slave states" and new "free states." By 1850 North and South reached a crossroads. At first Southern politicians refused to approve California to enter the Union as a new state. Finally, as part of the Compromise of 1850, both sides agreed to allow California's entry as a free state. Other states entering the Union would decide for themselves if they would be free or slave. The peace from this agreement did not last long.

The Kansas-Nebraska Act of 1854 allowed people in the two new territories to decide on the question of slavery. Nebraska voted to be free. But Kansas became a battleground between those who supported and opposed slavery. About 55 people were killed as violence broke out. People began calling the territory "Bleeding Kansas."

John Brown

In 1856 abolitionist John Brown and his followers killed a group of pro-slavery settlers in Kansas. Three years later, in 1859, he led a raid on the U.S. Army **arsenal** in Harpers Ferry, Virginia. He planned to take weapons to slaves. He hoped the slaves would form an army and win their own freedom.

Brown was captured and later hanged. But he became a symbol for both sides of the slavery issue. Some Northerners praised Brown as a hero. Southerners saw him as a villain.

arsenal—a place where weapons are stored

Cause #3
FIGHTING WORDS

THE LIBERATOR

Our Country is the World, our Countrymen are all Mankind.

BOSTON, FRIDAY, JULY 6, 1855.

In the 1850s and 1860s, Northerners and Southerners used increasingly harsh language when speaking and writing about the other group. Many historians agree that insults and name-calling deepened anger and resentment at the time.

For example, William Lloyd Garrison's abolitionist newspaper, *The Liberator*, called slave owners "evil savages." Garrison gave speeches accusing all Americans of being equally guilty in the eyes of God. He described in detail how slaves were sometimes beaten or killed. God would punish the nation for its wickedness, he said. He even called the U.S. Constitution "an agreement with hell" because it did not outlaw slavery. Many people in the 1800s took such religious comments very seriously.

In the 1850s Northern papers often called Southerners "barbarians," "violent traitors," and "ignorant." The same papers described people of the North as "mild," "moral," "peaceful," "humane," and "Christian." Southern books and papers called Northerners "mean spirited cowards" and "enemies of the peace." Southerners, on the other hand, were "noble," "kind," "polished," and "models of manners for the whole country."

Front page of *The Liberator*, an antislavery newspaper in 1855

Uncle Tom's Cabin

Harriet Beecher Stowe's novel *Uncle Tom's Cabin* helped change Northern attitudes about slavery. The story showed the cruelty of slave life. It also showed slaves as human beings with feelings, hopes, and dreams. More than 300,000 copies of the book were sold in 1852.

Brooks' cane attack nearly killed Sumner.

Even in the U.S. Congress personal attacks and insults became common. In 1856 Southern representative Preston Brooks beat Northern senator Charles Sumner with a cane at the U.S. Senate. Brooks did this because of a speech Sumner had made in Congress about the slavery question in Kansas. In that speech, Sumner condemned slavery and used crude language to describe Southerners. He even insulted a member of Brooks' family.

Southerners, of course, sided with Brooks. No Northerner should be allowed to insult the South, they said. Southerners even sent Brooks dozens of canes. Northerners saw the beating as proof that Sumner had spoken the truth about Southerners.

People traveled by wagon and on foot as they escaped to freedom on the Underground Railroad.

The Underground Railroad

The Fugitive Slave Act of 1850 increased Northern hatred against the South. It also increased activity on the Underground Railroad. Black and white abolitionists formed this network of safe homes and businesses to help runaway slaves escape to freedom. Railroad abolitionists provided food, money, and other goods. They also helped guide runaways to the next safe place—called a "station" or "depot." During the 1800s the Underground Railroad helped move hundreds of slaves north every year.

Cause #4

ABRAHAM LINCOLN AND THE ELECTION OF 1860

Few people had a greater impact on the Civil War than Abraham Lincoln. Lincoln's first real appearance on the national stage was in 1858. This was during his campaign against Stephen Douglas for the U.S. Senate seat in Illinois.

Douglas had first been elected senator in 1847. He helped pass the Compromise of 1850 and designed the Kansas-Nebraska Act of 1854.

Lincoln debated Douglas at Knox College in Galesburg, Illinois.

During this campaign, Lincoln spoke about the national debate over slavery this way:

"A house divided against itself cannot stand. I believe this government cannot endure, permanently half slave and half free. I do not expect the Union to be dissolved—I do not expect the house to fall—but I do expect it will cease to be divided. It will become all one thing or all the other."

Though Lincoln lost that Senate election, he gained attention for his antislavery stand. His clear determination to keep the Union together won him many supporters too.

But Lincoln stood for everything the South feared and hated. His statements that the nation could no longer be "half slave and half free" angered the South. Southerners were not about to let slavery end without a fight.

Lincoln ran as the Republican presidential candidate in 1860. Southern leaders made it clear that if Lincoln was elected, Southern states would **secede**. Southerners believed Lincoln's election would be a signal that the federal government would overpower Southern states. Southern states did not even put Lincoln on their ballots, but he won the election anyway.

After Lincoln's election, Southern states began seceding from the Union. South Carolina seceded first in December 1860, followed in 1861 by Mississippi, Florida, Alabama, Georgia, Louisiana, Texas, Virginia, Arkansas, North Carolina, and Tennessee. These states came together to form the Confederate States of America.

Lincoln made it clear that it would be up to Southerners to decide if war would come next. He said, "In your hands, my dissatisfied countrymen, and not in mine is the momentous issue of civil war."

But Lincoln's election had been the last straw. Southern leaders felt deeply offended by Northern leaders. People in the South followed an old and strict code of honor. In the old days, Southern white men fought duels if anyone insulted them or their families. Now tradition required them to react to the North's insults.

secede—to formally withdraw from a group or an organization, often to form another organization

FREE TERRITORY FOR A FREE PEOPLE.

A. LINCOLN.

H. HAMLIN.

An 1860 campaign banner for Abraham Lincoln
and his running mate, Hannibal Hamlin

A LONG AND BITTER STRUGGLE

The Confederates fired the first shots of the Civil War on April 12, 1861. It happened at Fort Sumter, a small Union fort in Charleston, South Carolina. Eighty-seven Union soldiers took shelter inside from the Confederate forces gathered outside. When the Union soldiers refused to surrender, the Confederates fired on the fort. Though the attack lasted about 33 hours, no one was killed or wounded. But the shots had begun the bloodiest war in U.S. history.

During four years of war, Union and Confederate armies fought hundreds of battles. Both sides suffered great losses in deadly battles such as Antietam, Chickamauga, Gettysburg, and Shiloh. Finally, on April 9, 1865, the war ended. Confederate General Robert E. Lee met Union General Ulysses S. Grant at Appomattox Courthouse, Virginia. There Lee signed the surrender of the South's main army to the North.

Fact

In 1863, in the midst of the war, President Lincoln released the Emancipation Proclamation. This order freed slaves in the rebellious states but Southerners refused to obey it. The Proclamation also allowed black troops to enter the Union military. By the end of the war, nearly 200,000 black soldiers and sailors had joined.

WHAT EFFECTS DID THE WAR HAVE ON AMERICA?

In many ways, people are still trying to make sense of the Civil War. One helpful way to understand the war is to study the effects it had on America.

The battles of the Civil War left many Southern states in ruin. Charleston, South Carolina, suffered great damage.

Effect #1

A Battered and Beaten South

The clearest effects of the war were felt in the defeated South. By 1865 Southern land was in ruins. When Confederate soldiers came home they found battered and broken cities. Many farms and plantations had been looted and burned. Fields once full of crops now lay bare and empty. People wandered about stunned and starving.

White Southern honor had taken a terrible beating. Few Southerners had believed they might lose the war. Now that they had, they were faced with a harsh reality. The old Southern idea of plantation life as the perfect kind of society was gone forever. Now blacks and whites were equal in the eyes of the law. Many white Southerners could not accept this idea. Some decided that, for them, the war was not over. They would hold on to the past and fight for as long as possible.

Millions of former slaves now had their freedom. But a life of freedom was a new and challenging experience. Many black people had no idea what to do, where to go, or how to make a living.

Many black people formed communities to help and support one another. Now they could freely start families and build real homes. Some began to search for separated family members. Women stayed home and cared for children instead of going into the fields to work. Blacks formed churches where they could freely gather to exchange information and find comfort.

After the war, the government tried to provide basic education and job training to former slaves.

Black communities recognized the power of knowledge. Slaves had been forbidden to learn how to read and write. But now black people could freely educate themselves and their children. During **Reconstruction,** the government created the Bureau of Refugees, Freedmen, and Abandoned Lands, better known as the Freedmen's Bureau. This agency set up schools for newly freed slaves, and blacks flocked to them. But the benefits of Reconstruction did not last very long.

Reconstruction—the period of time, following the Civil War, when the U.S. government tried to rebuild Southern states

During Reconstruction, Southern leaders strongly resisted help from the North. They did not like Northerners telling them what to do. And they hated the idea of any programs that might help blacks rise to equality with whites.

A member of the Freedmen's Bureau tries to stop groups of white and black Southerners from clashing.

Despite the leaders' resistance, some Northern aid still arrived in the South. The 12-year government program to help Southern states rebuild included sending workers and money. Many Northern volunteers tried hard to help people. The Freedmen's Bureau provided help to millions of poor Southerners. Black and white Southerners received food, clothing, shelter, medical care, and even schooling. No other federal program did more. But the Freedmen's Bureau did not get enough funding or last long enough to make a long-term impact.

Fact

Some dishonest Northerners tricked and cheated Southerners, particularly uneducated blacks, and stole a great deal of money. Southerners called these people "carpetbaggers" because of the luggage many of them carried.

White Southerners also faced a loss of political power. For many years, Southerners held great power in Washington. In America's short history as a nation, a majority of the presidents had been from the South. Most had been slave owners. For more than 40 years after 1869, all of America's presidents were from Northern states.

Under the Black Codes, black people in many states could be fined for being unemployed or homeless. Those who were unable to pay a fine could be forced to do hard labor instead.

But white leaders in the South still had local and state power. They used this power to respond to their fear of the newly freed black population. Seeing blacks' efforts to unite, whites reacted swiftly and often violently. Whites feared blacks would agree to work for less money and take jobs away from white people. States began to pass "Black Codes." These local rules took away rights from black citizens. In most states Black Codes kept blacks from freely buying, selling, or owning property. They prevented blacks from working certain jobs or serving on juries. In some states the laws also denied blacks the freedom to gather in large numbers or travel without special passes.

Effect #2
THE RISE OF JIM CROW

Congress passed new laws to protect the rights of blacks in the South. The Thirteenth Amendment, ratified in 1865, abolished slavery in the United States. The Fourteenth Amendment, ratified in 1868, gave citizenship and equal rights to freed slaves. The Fifteenth Amendment, added in 1870, made it illegal for any state to deny citizens the right to vote. But Southern leaders largely ignored these amendments, and nearly every Southern state found ways around the laws.

By the mid-1870s, Northern leaders had grown tired of dealing with the South. In 1877, President Rutherford B. Hayes ordered all federal troops out of Southern states. This officially ended Reconstruction. It also allowed white supremacy to continue growing stronger.

President Rutherford B. Hayes

Fact

Together, the Emancipation Proclamation and the Thirteenth, Fourteenth, and Fifteenth Amendments to the Constitution gave black men full rights as citizens. Women, however, were not allowed to vote until the Nineteenth Amendment was adopted in 1920.

The Black Codes continued, in spite of laws passed against them. Violent white supremacist groups such as the Ku Klux Klan terrorized blacks and anyone else who supported them.

The division between North and South grew. So did the division between blacks and whites. After 1877 the North and the federal government essentially turned their backs on black people. Another long and difficult period began for black Americans.

White supremacist groups used violence to stop blacks from voting, participating in business, and receiving an education.

The Jim Crow era began around the late 1870s. It was a new period of unjust rules and laws and poor treatment of blacks. It was named after Jim Crow, a cartoonish figure of a black person seen in popular plays.

Jim Crow was far more than just racial bullying. It was a system that made black people second-class citizens. Jim Crow laws kept blacks separate from whites in every part of daily life. Black children could not attend the same schools as white children. Black people could not vote, and most could not get better paying jobs, or even work beside whites.

The Jim Crow character made fun of black people and emphasized many negative stereotypes.

JIM CROW,
Pub. by Hodgson 10, Fleet Street & Turner & Fisher New York & Philadelphia

An engraving from 1850 shows a black man being told to leave a railroad car.

Some whites acted outside of the law to keep blacks down. Mobs threatened blacks with lynching. Lynching meant death by hanging, burning, or beating. Any black person who spoke or acted against a white person might be lynched. Many black people were lynched for no reason except to terrorize the black community. Lynching was a signal to black people to "stay in your place" and not try to change things.

For the next 80 years, Jim Crow locked blacks in a new kind of slavery—one of poverty and terror.

THE CIVIL RIGHTS MOVEMENT

The Jim Crow era in the South began to crumble in the 1950s and 1960s. At that time blacks began to demand the rights they had been denied for nearly 100 years.

The modern civil rights movement was a series of nonviolent protests and legal actions. People around the country began paying attention to the conditions most black Americans lived with every day. Southern white supremacists reacted with anger and violence. But Americans, white and black, united to fight for "liberty and justice for all."

In 1964 Congress passed the Civil Rights Act and President Lyndon B. Johnson signed it. This law completed work never finished after the Civil War. Other, tougher laws followed. Complete equality could not happen overnight. But America was finally becoming a fairer place for all people.

President Lyndon B. Johnson

Modern Effects of the Civil Rights Movement

Speaking in Austin, Texas, on April 10, 2014, President Barack Obama said:

"Because of the civil rights movement, because of the laws President Johnson signed, new doors of opportunity and education swung open for everybody—not all at once, but they swung open... They swung open for you, and they swung open for me. And that's why I'm standing here today."

As the civil rights movement went on, people all over the United States protested for equal rights.

Effect #3

Growing Industry and the Gilded Age

The Civil War led to a new time of business and growth in the United States. The war proved that industry was far more profitable than agriculture. After all, the factories of the North had beaten the plantations of the South.

Even before the war ended, Congress passed laws that encouraged more industry and settlement. The Homestead Act of 1862 sent millions of settlers west to claim free land in new territories. Pacific Railway Acts of 1862 and 1864 started railroad building west of the Mississippi River.

The federal government provided land and money to encourage western railroad construction.

Andrew Carnegie became one of the richest men of the Gilded Age by helping to build the American steel industry.

After the war, business and industry boomed. Because a few people made huge amounts of money, the period became known as the **Gilded** Age. Millionaires such as John D. Rockefeller, Andrew Carnegie, and Cornelius Vanderbilt became household names. Many of these **tycoons** began making their fortunes during the war. Their shops and factories provided weapons, wagons, uniforms, and thousands of other war supplies. After the war, growing industry made America an ever-stronger world power.

gilded—covered with a thin layer of gold
tycoon—a rich and powerful business person

Effect #4
THE GROWTH OF THE NEWS MEDIA

Before the war, "news" meant stories that were mostly local and not very up to date. But during the war people wanted the newest facts. The invention of high-speed printing presses and the telegraph in the 1830s made faster reporting possible. Information could be sent hundreds or thousands of miles in seconds. Super-fast printing machines could make thousands of papers in minutes. The number of newspapers skyrocketed. Every large city had several papers. Most small towns had at least one.

Some writers took on the new job of war correspondent, talking to soldiers on the battlefield. War photography also grew during the Civil War. Newspapers of the Civil War era are still a major tool for historians today. Words and pictures of the time help us better understand not just what happened but why.

A Civil War era newspaper shows a torpedo exploding in a naval battle.

A war correspondent for the political magazine *Harper's Weekly* sketches near the battlefield at Gettysburg.

CONCLUSION

President Lincoln was assassinated by an angry Southerner just days after the Confederate surrender. He had succeeded in preserving the Union, but hundreds of thousands of men died in the process. Before his death, Lincoln spoke about the need to "bind up the nation's wounds." It would take decades for Americans to recover from the war, but the United States had been changed forever.

GLOSSARY

abolitionist (ab-uh-LI-shuhn-ist)—a person who worked to end slavery before the Civil War

arsenal (AR-suh-nuhl)—a place where weapons are stored

compromise (KAHM-pruh-myz)—to agree to something that is not exactly what you wanted in order to make a decision

fugitive (FYOO-juh-tiv)—someone who has escaped from prison or slavery

gilded (GIL-ded)—covered with a thin layer of gold

plantation (plan-TAY-shun)—a large farm found in warm areas; before the Civil War, plantations in the South used slave labor

Reconstruction (ree-kuhn-STRUHKT-shuhn)—the period of time, following the Civil War, when the U.S. government tried to rebuild Southern states

secede (si-SEED)—to formally withdraw from a group or an organization, often to form another organization

tycoon (tye-KOON)—a rich and powerful business person

white supremacy (WITE suh-PREM-a-see)—the idea that the white race is superior to all other races

READ MORE

Bader, Bonnie. *Who Was Robert E. Lee?* New York: Grosset & Dunlap, an imprint of Penguin, 2014.

Cocca, Lisa Colozza. *Reconstruction and the Aftermath of the Civil War.* Understanding the Civil War. New York: Crabtree Pub. Co., 2012.

Fitzgerald, Stephanie. *The Split History of the Civil War.* Perspectives Flip Books. North Mankato, Minn.: Compass Point Books, 2013.

Nardo, Don. *A Nation Divided: The Long Road to the Civil War.* The Civil War. Mankato, Minn.: Compass Point Books, 2011.

Wittman, Susan S. *Heroes of the Civil War.* The Story of the Civil War. North Mankato, Minn.: Capstone Press, 2015.

CRITICAL THINKING USING THE COMMON CORE

1. President Abraham Lincoln died April 15, 1865. How might Reconstruction in the South have been different if Lincoln had lived? (Integration of Knowledge and Ideas)

2. How did the idea of white supremacy encourage slavery as well as the Jim Crow era following the Civil War? (Key Ideas and Details)

3. How might America be different today if the Civil War had not been fought? Use other sources to support your answer. (Integration of Knowledge and Ideas)

INTERNET SITES

FactHound offers a safe, fun way to find Internet sites related to this book. All of the sites on FactHound have been researched by our staff.

Here's all you do:

Visit *www.facthound.com*

Type in this code: 9781491420096

INDEX